MILES PRESS

Indiana University South Bend Department of English

MOUTH

42 Miles Press
Editor, David Dodd Lee
Copyright© 2015 Tracey Knapp. All rights reserved.
ISBN 978-0-9830747-8-6 (pbk. alk. paper)

For permission, required to reprint or broadcast more than several lines, write to:
42 Miles Press, Department of English, Indiana University South Bend
1700 Mishawaka Avenue, South Bend, IN 46615

http://42miles.wordpress.com

Art Direction: Nicholas Kuder, Design: Sam DeLoof, Production: Paul Sizer
The Design Center, Frostic School Of Art, Western Michigan University.
Printing: McNaughton & Gunn, Inc.

MOUTH

POEMS
BY
TRACEY
KNAPP

CONTENTS

II.

III.

For my mother, Nancy Szmurlo Knapp

And for my father, Gary Knapp (1943-2009)

I.

It becomes still more difficult to find
Words at once true and kind,
Or not untrue and not unkind.
—Phillip Larkin

ENTROPY

All those times I crossed the bridge to see you
and not one lap dance. We haven't held hands
since that time in the rain forest, chanting Lord
knows what in Sanskrit. I saw my first wild boar there
but even he took off for the brush. Someone always ends
the moment. Another call dropped on your iPhone,
the cosmic forces at work. My dog sighs and stares
at my flip-flop from his pillow. At work, the office
is separated into orderly earth-toned cubes.
My friends, we gather here today
to sit exactly ten feet apart. I am exactly
one hour away from being drunk enough
to call my psychic in Tuscaloosa, two
commercials away from another headache
and *Nova* on TV. The universe expands, shifting
its contents accordingly. There was a time
when we were closer. Helen Keller learned to speak
by holding her teacher's face, feeling the words form
and fall out of her mouth, her throat buzzing with thought.
I also like to touch people while they talk,
but not about professional sports. I love
and hate eye contact, don't you? One glance
from the Girl Scout and I buy the Thin Mints. I don't get
all that crap about divine connection,
but there is something to be said for
a collective consciousness if you consider how
everyone likes vampires again. If I had a spirit
animal, I think it would be the wild boar.
We never talk about it anymore and I miss that
about us. The only thing that could prevent
a greater distance forming between two stars

hurtling through space would be some entropic net,
a giant wet towel. While you're crossing
the state line on your last gallon of gas,
a streetlight deteriorates over the Safeway
parking lot. A shopping cart rolls
into my Dog Chow and the bag splits
wide open, the pellets skidding and colliding
across the pavement, two strangers scrambling
to gather them, to fill the bag together, to make it right.

DIFFICULTIES

I fell asleep in the grocery line while
waiting to buy you a ham. I was waiting
for the right moment to tell you.
I told you about my first time in
Cincinnati, the man on the bus
who smelled of formaldehyde.
I can still feel his wool jacket
scratching against my bare arm.
I can barely feel my fingers.
It's so cold that the whiskers
on my dog look like icicles. We
are walking towards the sun's last
attempt. The snow is stacked high
but my dog begins digging like there's
an enormous flank steak beneath,
and what does he pull up but his old
squeaky whale! We hadn't seen it
since summer. It's been a difficult winter.
It's been difficult to smoke pot
with my accountant. He tells me
it's not the sixties, and it's not the first
time I've heard that. The first time I heard
about your sick cat, I tried to call but
I heard you were turning yourself
into a grain of sand. I have turned
you into a grain of sand.
This is the first time I can honestly
say that. The first glass of wine
was followed by the next and now
it's the first Monday at this new
desk, the first Monday I haven't spent
the evening loathing my thighs
over a glass of wine. Where there's
self-loathing, there's yourself,
and then the one bright thing
underneath that makes life
worth digging for.

TOLD YOU SO

today I will consider your point about the lemon
how it stops the opened flesh of fruit from spoiling
how its rind keeps the leaves of basil soft in the freezer

there's always something I could do better
like the way I hold cats or clean the bathtub
but I'm not concerned with every improvement

the lesson I had was about splinters
if you ignore them how they fester
and the electrocution of walking on them

but you got so impatient with my tweezers
I could never get it out and then
it was my fault at the doctor's

you were right about envelopes
and everything you said on fruit flies
has proven to be true

you did admit the old adage of
absence makes the heart is total crap
we can agree on that together

I have said before I listen best in situations
of great tension such as I am right and you are wrong
or I don't like old salad I don't care what you say

and there I am later buying lemons
squeezing them over lettuce then waiting
for the leaves to wilt in spite of myself

APOLOGY

There was a glass on the windowsill. I broke it.
A song you liked about a paddleboat, a baby boy.
I refused to sing it. I did not eat the eggs you made,
your brittle toast. I feared I wouldn't like the taste
and so I chose not to act. I'm actively sorry.
I cannot hold you. There are cats on your mattress
to console you. When you woke up on the train
your backpack was gone again. It's probably okay
to blame me. There is a storm cloud stirring
over Toledo for which I am likely accountable.
And also for the splinters in your fist, the bitchy fence
that bore my resemblance. There is a lamppost
leaning towards the ground, its light long gone.
A moth that has given up. The month
of June is polluted with the disappointment
of empty bottles, the spoiled hope of plump
tomatoes. It will be hard for you to ever feel
full again. It will be hard for you to forgive me.

STEALING

Kent stole a sports coat from the Big and Tall

and Lucy lifted a gentleman's monocle at the antique fair

She says sometimes she steals because no one is watching

I saw a homeless guy steal some Slim Jims, but I didn't tell

Tom believes there is a difference between stealing from Jake at the corner store

versus batteries at Walmart, which he has done for years

I agree with him that it's less personal when your victim is a corporate entity

but the homeless guy was just drunk and hungry, and Tom is a smug asshole

My brother stole a duck phone from a police station once

when it rang, it quacked

and also a guitar strap from a Sonic Youth concert in 1993

I went to court for a Bob Marley tape I took from the record store when I was seventeen

My father was a cop, so you can imagine my humiliation

I swore, never again, but then there was the half-moon pendant at the River Fest

You'd think they would know better, keep an eye on the small stuff

Watch the things that matter most and trust no one

but then there goes some dickhead with my backpack

and his new box of tampons, eyelash curler, an anthology of Japanese feminist poetry

FLOOD DAMAGE

The wormy dolor of downpour
wears through the dirt. Wetter
than water. Like going under,

we hold breath, hurry towards the door.
A globe of branches floats outside our window,
whirling in unruly waters. I pile towels

on the puddled floor. No one
is thirsty anymore. Powerless,
we fidget and burn

candles in the kitchen. Nothing left
to say to one another. Holed up home,
the world is tinier than we

can fathom. Smaller, I fear, than all these rooms
where we go differently in the streaming dark,
the sound of rain pounding louder than heart.

LOVER WALKING

You leave me in bed
to note the sunrise from
my garden, buy me
coffee with seven quarters
at the corner store.

You sell sweatshirts on your front lawn,
take pennies from the city fountains.

You're busking for dollars
in the Rockridge Station,
singing Sloop John B
off-key on the escalator,
your voice shameless and bright.

No job will have you—
no matter.

You are in love.
You write me a note on an oak leaf
with a pigeon feather.

You are loud in quiet places—
crying on the park bench,
yelling in the tulips.

You are drunk again,
kneeling in the gravel.

Always you either want
to live or die.

You, with a whistle and a cigarette,
a story about stealing and a sigh.

You, with grease stains on your jacket,
inconsolable on the last train home.

Moving past the slatted fence,
moving over me:
your body a rhythm of light.

You kissed me in the rain
on our first and last nights,
like the rain opened and closed on us.
Like we were a book of rain.

I SAID YOU SAID

When you said that
you were taking the keys
from the house
I thought you were mad about
the broken phone, the dead gerbil
after another night of alarming length
in our cluttered bedroom
I thought you meant
you were leaving me
the television

I thought you meant
you were escaping
and locking the door behind you
your car stalling in the road
you couldn't revive it
repairing what was broken
was pointless
you wouldn't be back
so I hurled
out the window

BIG DEAL, SMALL TOWN

Bonjour, as they say in Paris.
Hello, you're in Dubuque.
You're finally home,

after crossing state lines
like a razor blade across
a crisp new map. Everyone

is in the kitchen, waiting
for you. Everyone remembers
the last time you were here,

drinking water from the hose.
Back then, you could get away
with knee socks. You could turn

a cricket into a field mouse
back then, you were just
that good. I can't actually

remember anything bad about you,
it's been that long.
We've missed you

in proximity, having your body
as close as the fern you planted
outside your bedroom window

when you were five.
Back then, I used to call you
Fern. Your back, the side

we see too much of,
or not enough.
Turn around and come closer,

I want to stroke your arm
with a feather. Does that tickle?
Does it float away in the breeze?

CECI N'EST PAS UNE PIPE
—after Magritte

This is not Dunhill, Ferndown, nor the White Bar Castello.
Not corncob nor deer bone, Ser Jacopo.

Do not light that which you perceive
to be an opening.

Latakia, Cavendish,
the dark-stoved Virginias;
Perique will dry and crumble.
Nothing burns with pleasure.

Do not mistake the smoldering within to be self-contained
for it can spread like a shiver in the ashen streets.
There is no comfort taken from a hazy reed.
This is not a pipe.

Therefore, you can breathe with velvet asperity.
Therefore, your hands smell of lavender.

There are no immediate pleasures.
Your oral fixation: unfulfilled.
The tongue remains unnumb.

This is not the wood of pulverized burl,
this ink is no rare tar of smoke and spices.
This will burn like a sheet of shaven birch.

Sea, see nay poison peep.

Nothing escapes.
Nothing gets better in the end.

We sway and moan.
Oh, Holy Pipe.
We were not made in your likeness.

TO THE NEW MOON

Come night. Come
sirens and midnight babies
born in the backseats
of taxicabs. Come moon.

You crazy weeping
alcoholic, quit drinking
yourself into nothingness.
Someone's trumpet
has gone missing tonight.

Someone is looking
for you, holding your
hairbrush to the nose
of a bloodhound.

Leave your shadow
on the door mat
and come inside. I'll cook
you up something good,
a grilled cheese sandwich
to go with that frown.

It's just us girls
tonight. Let's spray paint
the stairwell, burn
phonebooks in the bathtub.

Even though you're telling me
you're done, it's over, I've still hung
my clothes out to dry overnight
in the ocean wind, and that tide

is all your work. You may
have been the first,
but you're not the only one
to circle your grief, to slowly
darken because of it.

I know that it's hard to show
your face in the face
of the sun and his narcissism,
the earth's pushy shadow,
but I've seen you in the daylight,
edging into the sky
early for a while, urging

the herons to stab at fish,
the street cars to lurch
up and over the long hill
before they rattle on down towards the bay.

Moon, it's two in the morning
and it's time to stop hiding:
the French Alps are talking
about your new glow,
how you actually look younger,
and all the dogs adore you.

INHERITANCE

I've been checking on your cats as you asked,
watering the plants that have since outgrown
their rotting baskets, and just today I noticed the skin

of mold on the old pot of coffee.
It reminded me of the field of algae on the pond out back
beyond the ruined railroad ties of this place,

once our grandma's house where her dogs
uprooted deer bones and nuzzled each other's butts
under a dim swarm of bees choking themselves

on pollen. We used to walk there in the faltering
light and we pretended you were the mother
who let me sleep on the rocks and eat dirt.

I was always in your context—me, the shy one,
you with the freckled lips, your saggy hand-me-down
swimsuits—how our father loved you so effortlessly.

Remember when it downpoured and we were still up
in the old oak, the thunder throwing us around?
I might have cried or screamed in fear but there you were,

your large eyes electric with thrill, your fist
holding mine as the wet leaves stuck to our thighs.
How I was just your little sister then, not the weird one

who defined your own beauty through its subtle distortion,
a chromosomal snag in the family silk.
Never mind the blackberry thorns still stuck

in my palms from a little shove at the pricker bush.
Whatever. Nothing could fix my sullen face
like your hand pulling me over the neighbors' fence,

us both falling backwards into the waist-high grass.
Later, I loved your quiet devotion to my ankle
as you tweezed a drunken tick. Its ballooned body

popped between your fingers and we gasped at the blood.
Sometimes I followed you out back while our parents slept.
Your teenage boyfriend hauled the rotting logs,

threw them on the fire. Do you remember lying
down in the leaves and telling me to get lost?
Which I always sort of did—your voice

lowly murmuring me away, your hair bright and full,
the light of the shimmering embers, his tan body
arching over you... Sisters can make you feel so

small sometimes. Older now, and I'm still
exaggerating our differences: your chirpy laugh,
my combat boots. But despite your perfect breasts,

I can still sit out here on the lawn and drink the last
of the beer you left since he slipped you into his white Cadillac,
a giant envelope on softened wheels ripping down

the dirt roads and off into something like a sunset.
I have since waited for you past the stars rising and the days
have dropped down before me, asked me knee-bent:

what do I own and who owns my life? I beg myself
for something other than my own words to answer: the crickets'
cyclic hymn, your hands braiding my hair behind me.

ON LOSS

I have been thinking too much about the blue cap I lost, somewhere between

your house and the fountain in front of City Hall, where a blind woman washed

her feet that day in late March. When the soap slipped out of her hands, we didn't

say anything, which is probably why I lost my hat if you believe in karma,

which is probably why I lost grasp of your hand during the parade,

there were so many other people in pirate costumes. One pirate's loss,

another pirate's chest of coins. Blackbeard once left his favorite

bandolier on a bucket outside a bar in Charleston, but the boy watching

him pee against the hitching post didn't speak up, pawned the belt

at some pig farm outside town. They both lost big in the end,

just like all of us, another boat cannonballed then seized by the sea.

Everyone watches some ship sink, everyone slows down on the highway

to look at the crash, the contents of the trunk blowing into the brush,

the paramedics pulling a cart down into the ditch.

Another stranger died today. Another stranger remembered

me as Stacy, bought me an awkward martini. I'm also terrible

with names. What have I forgotten to deserve that? The mailman

forgets about me on Sundays, you remind me to send in my taxes. You

remind me of a man I saw once in Ohio on my way to buy corn.

It was a Sunday, a funeral emerging from the only church

I remember there, the air tight with frost. There was a horse

on the lawn. The man moved slowly, inspecting the grass, arms shrugged

into his jacket, then lifted something blue—a hat—from a bald shrub,

studied it with all the fingers of both his hands and then carefully set it back.

TRUST ME

I would never hurt you, at least
not today. Just about any time
after four tomorrow would be okay.
I will be waiting naked at the door.

I will be waiting on the floor with
a sock puppet and a cardboard box
as a stage. I'm writing a one-scener,

a short play. It's either called
Pretty Little Pickaxe or *I'll Bite You*
If You Stay. How long will this take?

I don't stick around for pain,
not the kind that scars, anyway,
at least not on my face. I trust you

brought the incriminating audio tape,
the heavy breathing from last Tuesday,
a confession involving a garden rake.

I lied about bronchitis, lied about the lamp
I never really gave to the neighbors,
its lame stem leaning into the trash can
like the cracked neck of a dead crane.

You don't believe me? I don't blame you.
I never tell anyone about our sex play,
or at least, I never mention

your name. You could be anybody. Which is
why I'm boss in this game, the kind
of boss who would never fire you, more like

the kind with a horsewhip and a bullhorn.
More like a muzzle than a chain.
Come over. I've been waiting all day.

There's a bottle of wine on the counter
that we might never open, that might be better
broken. There's trouble written all over
my face.

RED EYE

The woman sitting beside me
just pulled her bra out from
her sleeve and I'm thinking
that's not a bad idea, a little release
from the strain of the day.

It's time to dim the cabin lights,
time to quiet the constant inner chatter,
the terrifying uncertainties of flight and also
this uncertain life, time to take off
my sneakers and make the best
of this window seat, a song
on my headphones about collapsing
stars. I heard a prediction
of the earth getting hit
by a giant comet in 2029,
the massive tsunami that follows,
swallowing my entire city
and then spitting it
back out. The plane
hiccups over an invisible bump.

Maybe they were right
about the apocalypse,
although I never thought I
would live to see it.
Maybe I will never live
to see the next *Star
Magazine*, or learn
the truth about UFOs,
but I am pretty sure that

I don't care about crop circles
or celebrity cellulite. I don't care
about a lot of things anymore, but
I am going to start caring about
myself again, right now,
and then build up
a dedicated following.

I'm going to stop hovering
over dark matter, flirting
with the black hole
of hang-ups and hangovers.

I'm going to fit into
those checkered shorts again,
I'm going to make out
with my hot neighbors
and I'm going to start
eating early dinners.

Oh, late night burgers!
It's only midnight
but I am ready for my
second bag of salted peanuts
and another Xanax.

I can't relax when I consider
the man who loves me
even though he should know
better, my little snits
and silences escalating
our tension to a fearful height.

The woman with the bra
has rested her head
on my shoulder, her snore
like the purr of an elderly cat,
slow and staggered.
The clouds ramble by
in inconsistent fits. From
35,000 feet, I can see a city
below me flickering like
a miniature galaxy
in the shape of a crescent,
spooning itself around
some dark lake.

PERFECT OBJECTS

Perhaps it is true that you are lost,
your aimless job shucking oysters,
another love going nowhere fast,
another wrong turn off the freeway
that takes you the wrong way down
the wrong road. Where are you going?
Even the kitchen mouse has more direction
than you, moving up in life from the flax seed
to the cat food. The cat glowers
from the corner, counting each pellet.
You glower at the sous chef
who is in grad school for archeology—
what the hell is he going to do with
that? What the fuck with his pride?
You should know—you, with your degree
in geography, your own fascination
with rock formations. What perfect objects.
How you can always find them
again. How they stand still for so long
in one position, like it's their only job.

LAST LAUGH

outside of the bar you laughed over how funny it was when I stormed out and then there were no taxis

I can't remember what you did but it only meant I wouldn't be coming over

one cab finally pulled up and neither of us could bear to take it, be the first person to leave

nor find funny how sad it is to be the last one standing there

the jerk with the mouth who gets to go home alone

so I just walked, took the scenic route

past the collapsing barn, all of the shoes on the telephone wire

and how many lights on in all of the kitchens, someone unable

to sleep next to the person asleep in their bed

and the moths in August on the streetlamps

bumping faithfully into the light

the crickets with the crunch of shoes

against fresh gravel, the new tar cooking

and I thought if I wasn't alone I wouldn't have noticed the moon

but then after two miles back to the house, the dog in the pen

was asleep and crowding the tree stump with her body

WHILE YOU WAIT

I thought *yes the striped one* when
you had to choose between two shirts.
Our clothes always on the floor,
our headlights only on low beam in this city,

tonight as foggy as when I had a place
in San Francisco where I took
the bus and knew the bars that opened up
at 6 a.m., my ears still ringing

from the thrust of bass, the drag queen/nurse
offering me lines in the ladies' room. That was
then. This is how I spell your name phonetically.
Now I know the hairs that root around the oblation

of your nipple like I could draw your fingerprint
blind. I like your eyes, your hands are cold.
May I kiss you? You may lie to me
when I tell you I'm afraid of truth beforehand.

You can do anything. I haven't named your legs yet,
your mouth remains a separate math.
What do you think of my eyelids, my lips pale
as dead? I have been waiting days, months even.

Hurry up, I'm starving. Put on the shirt, drink down
the glass, put up with how I ride the clutch at stoplights.
I am trying to get there faster, driving fast
to where we can't be closer.

You're being patient. I can tell that.

II.

*I heard words
and words full
of holes
aching. Speech
is a mouth.*

—Robert Creeley

MAGNETIA

My pulsing iris:
what pulls
you now?
The charm of lip:
chump change
to this.

His torso
wider than deep,
more diagonal
than that.
I'm dizzy over
hair, a fan
of his combing.

Damn desire.
I can't stop staring.
Starry and falling, I am
forward-sinking
and seeing more
than something.

Looking is
like licking.
The one time
I can't talk.
A clock, a face, I'm
noon, an *oh oh*, an
exultation that lacks
language. Excision
of my mouth.

ACTION TAKEN

blamed the Glen Livet and the Vicodin on you

fell off a bar stool but climbed right back up

pushed a shopping cart into a rack of wine

pissed like a dog in the field where we'd tangled

spit glass into my hands during fifty Hail Marys

misspelled your name backwards across the front of an ambulance

pet named you Splinter, then Bullet Hole

whittled the driftwood we took from the beach into a little thorn

mailed you a cat bone and pictures of my newest bruises

heated your pendant on the neighbor's grill

wore it for weeks to hide its own burn

called you My Little Liar to whoever would listen

took my own boot to my face and then kicked it

sneezed blood for a week and forgot your scent

removed the tattoo of your hand on my ass

sucked lemons daily to keep this face

collapsed in a crosswalk, woke up in your driveway

smoked opium while prostitutes stroked my throat

bet your diamond on a horse named The Next Best Thing

found you the perfect coffin, darling

skulked around with a hammer and a fistful of nails

WHO CALLS YOU

Inventor of the Honey Extractor in the Great Farms of Bees
Farmer of Edible Flowers
Farmer in a Field of Cherubs
Wanderer, Walker of Ancient Footpaths
The One Who Recycles the Gas Pans of Retired Automobiles
Stranger Appearing Beside You Again at the Traffic Light
Crucible Uncracked, Door Hinge, Fingerprint
The Sixth Finger of the King's Second Wife
Baby's First Swear Word and Other Memorable Curses
The One Frog You'll Never Forget
Three Forgotten Hours on Some Montana Highway
New Freckle: Found
Top Ten Facial Expressions for Awe
Match Book, Blinker, Invisible Hammer
Inventor of the Complicated Machine
Harbinger of Diminishing Gravity
Harnesser of Human Gasps and Gaping Jaws
Little Bubble of Sunlight Reflecting Off the Kitchen Floor
Floater Above the Heads of Others
Inexplicable Presence in Unlit Sheds
The Taste on our Tongues in Darkening Fields of Goldenrod:

Please erase my name
from your lists of
The Discontented,
The Once-Loved
and Those Allergic to Cats.
I have renamed
the stop sign
"Little Kismet"
and promise
to fix my brakes.

E.D.

May 15th (an anniversary)

Dear Editor,

    Upon your request, I am not sending you another poem about my mother. I am not sending along a long poem about her; she also requested that I not send you such poems. She also requested I give it a rest. She, as you know, was once more vocal. Her tongue, a rusty razor, once rolled with laughter.

Where are *her* poems, you probably wonder? Wasn't she one girl with a probable poem? A conceit, a secret sonnet, a love poem, a letter? Let her send her bitter songs herself. Why does her daughter keep sending you poems? I think it is because she says I have no real talent. "Miss D.," you will say, "your talent is evident, but I cannot publish your Mother Poems. I wouldn't mind seeing your mother's, if she has any poems."

This is the last poem, upon your request. Upon her request this is the last.

Respectfully, respectively
Yours, my mother's,

Her Daughter

IN THE SHAPE OF A MAN

Nothing short of delicious
was the case. A sense of
midgetry informed the piece,
a smallish whip of mousse
atop the cute forehead.
I ate the feet first,
his green shoes a smart
mint taste. My tongue
shivered fresh. I liked
the buttons best, a metallic
look and hard to bite.
I didn't lose a tooth.
After the arms and waist,
crumbs scattered
over my new suede.
Still, I relished the final parts,
the look on his face.

BLONDE

lipstick on the cucumbers   she couldn't keep her calves together

male gets delivered to the right box   she wasn't used to being in the front seat

bite marks on the steering wheel   why was she upset

when her tampon is behind her ear   she can't find her pencil   fired from her job

why did the blonde fail   call the welfare office   jump off a bridge

drive into the ditch   why did she scale the chain-link fence   break her leg

marks on her back   how did the blonde explain   have another beer

other guys waiting their turn   the more you bang it

how many does it take to screw   a blonde at a flashing red light

crawling across the street   when is it legal to shoot a blonde in the head

couldn't dial 911   when she wakes up on the floor

she gets dressed and goes home

THE CHAIRS ARE ON THE TABLE

I wish I had the chance to say
Oh, little life, you unpolished spoon!
but I'm afraid that this is not the poem.

Don't expect a jar of fireflies here,
no sexual orchids or doorways of importance,
no moths over candlelight.

There won't be an ocean
so no looking down in it
and definitely no drowning.

However, I hope you find
the absence of children refreshing.
Also, there are no understated bullet wounds.
Sometimes irony is terrifying.

Perhaps you would comment on fear
in an explication of this poem.
Maybe a revision would result
in the deletion of all speculative adverbs.

I can say for sure
the speaker is aware of her contradictions.
Nonetheless, she is committed
to representing the truth as accurately as possible:

she wanted to end with the line
Today I mopped the floor vigorously and it's still dull
but afraid there's more to it,
she'd rather not consider the floor

needs more mopping—
a new mop entirely.

EMERGENCY EXIT

Out on the fire
escape the rainwater
darts between the iron slats
then falls in larger form
upon the black
umbrellas that clot
the crosswalks.

Taxis crash
through the runoff
and heave
their muddied bodies
to the curbs, to the streets
and curbs again.

The fuse is blown and so
nothing—
no spark to enflame
us nor need to let the ladder
down. It's something of
a hush, but don't call this
silence—for which chord
would you choose to choke
among the others?

The sirens desist.
Let this last light fall
away, its winter
whimper sad as some
mouthless dirge,
all moan and tears.

CALM

Imagine this poem bordered by doves.
Doves are meant to pacify.

This is the calm of one dove's death:
a corpse, no longer clawing for life.

This is the beast, the fox after the kill.
After the feast, his rest, his exhale.

The slugs' and maggots' smooth ride
over the rotting body. Their indulgence.

And then the crows: let them devour the carcass,
consume the flesh and maggots whole.

This is the tree they return to at night.
Hundreds perch like winter leaves.

The center root of the oldest birch
driving down into the cold dark dirt.

Through the loam, the dense organic.
The great waste, the once-life. Earth.

WHAT WIND HOLDS HIM

indirect fire and you're under the bed again   yank on the flak jacket   good morning

mosquitoes at your ankles   the coarse floor scuffing your chinbone   dirt gathering in your boots

in your beaten locker   crayon drawings of butterflies   circle above a printout

your daughter's face covered in yams   here the children will not go outside with their torn dolls

to where the flies hover   you will never see dogs in the same way   their indiscriminate snouts

rooting around the bombed mosque for the dead   you will never walk

down a city street   without flinching from the sound of sirens

but you have slept through the shrieking nights   four less men the next morning

you know of someone   sent home in two shipments   you know of someone

who just arrived   no crud yet creasing his cheeks

good morning   the only bird you've seen in months   a buzzard

what wind holds him in this ruined sky   grimed with oil and gun powder

you know of only one thing   you can do to make him stop circling

POWERS THAT BE

We forgot to tell you about
the new threshold for pain.
We apologize for the inconvenience.
We are flogging the proletariat
and will leave them with
everything they brought
to the yard sale to sell.
We will buy nothing. Nothing
gets better in the future,
it only becomes a larger
version of itself. Or smaller,
but more complicated,
a microchip the size
of a pen tip. Are you writing
this down? We have
eaten twenty-seven percent
of your homemade jam,
twelve percent of your
pudding. Our constituents
have readied the ballot boxes,
and they're keeping your seat
warm with the mayor's Pomeranians.
Another bar filled
with your frenemies, drunk
on schnapps and hungry for war
coverage on the widescreen.
We loiter at the door but don't
bother going in. We are
paying the price for it,

in muscles. An artificially
inflated price, we never really
had to work out. We were born
with this body. We were not born
into poverty. We have risen
up from the dreary beds
of the great and ancient ones
and now we are going
to whoop
your ass.

BAD MOOD, BAKER BEACH

Just told some dude with a poodle to fuck off.

My pound mutt humped his puppy's ass.

He pretends to call the cops. No answer and I knew it.

Bigger problems in this town.

I will never understand the appeal of anger.

So bored. Weather exhausts me. You call this winter?

I'll show you winter. Tea kettle spilled over door locks.

Hot shovel from the wood stove. Ashes, pitfall.

The water here is always bitter cold.

Big tease. Did I mention I am allergic to wet suits?

So much for surfing. Might as well move back East,

land of snow and warm summer water. Might be better

than sitting on a cold beach, staring at a red bridge

they never stop painting. What's the point? All of this beauty

everywhere. So stupid. My wet dog licks my cheek, shakes

out the water from his fur all over me.

Dumb sun, set already. This sucks. Sand in my socks.

I will never be happy.

THE EDGE OF THE EARTH

My thanks for your hospitable grip,
the muffle of my downward *ohhh*.
I write to say I have not yet splattered.

I have not bitten the dust, or otherwise
choked on it. You've let me plummet
in peace and for that, in thanks, may I release
this bottle rocket for you? May the sparks

tickle in ricochet. Let the dark floor
of your basement be lit up
with my controlled explosives.
May it be padded with enormous hands.

Hold me up, Rock Bottom,
Broad Crest Opposing Starry Vastness!
Face the moon, that skull, that Bleak Face
of Nothingness. Lift me up so I may

slap it, cup it, kiss the Nothing
dumb and girlishly, the goat in me gone
to pasture, my nose grazing the great lawn
beyond your expanding chasm.

LEAVING LAND

pirates shmirates—let's cross the ocean

we'll unhitch a schooner fast at night

sail south or west, away from land

its maddening gridlock where we squabble

in August hotness over which lane or who gets the bike

the dog on board can be named Matey

his rear left leg made of a teak post

you do the fishing and I'll worry about oranges

not about when we'll find time for walking

Matey gets the small fish, curls at our feet

when we sleep on the deck on the quiet nights

water splashing against the hull will often surprise us

you can be the boat and I'll be the water

I'll come over the hull disguised

as a flash storm, an unfathomable wave, as Surprise

as the Lack of Expectation

you'll be the Time After Everything Was Going as Planned

and at that minute when our moments meet

we won't be undertowed, landlocked, body-bound

but the compound escaping impossible ground

TANGLE

Blossom or knot, the gather
        of petal or cord contains an inner
layer, a fold dark as fist. As if a lesson
            in privacy, the strays cluster under cars
in the snow, their tails flickering
            at the wheels. Two lovers whisper
within the tent of their covers.
            Too coiled to say *these are my hands,*
these are my toes. This inextricable
            bind implies some kind of interior
entente. So often we go where we cannot
            see parts of ourselves: in every fissure,
you'll find two walls tight and close.
            Always the line is black, some pressure
pushing together or pulling apart.
            That close, you never know.

PACKING IT UP

You, with a handle on things, your vacuum
snorting the last dust from the corners of the den,
how easily pleased you were to clean a
home you wouldn't remember living in.

You scalped the ornamented shelves
with one quick swipe and the ballerinas,
the miniature lambs, shattered against
your swoop. The paint boys spackled
the nail holes, lacquered over your childhood
in one flat eggshell coat.

The town came to shop and see what had been
hidden in the old house. The yard, trashed
with keepables: some televisions, a mica lamp,
your bassinet. The beautiful neighbor misheld
your old bassoon, but you stood back,
admiring her manicure.

In the end, you filled your car
with picture albums, commemorative plates,
and the clothes you took to Goodwill.
A garbage truck came to get the dumpster
the next day. And you, with a handle on things,
left the houseplants scorching on the lawn.

NO ANSWER

Why is the bag lady yelling at her coffee?
Why is that man smoking on my fire escape?
Angela, you seem so far today. You could explain
the falconer on the back porch talking to the jays.
You will always have answers. A fat pigeon wobbles
in front of a moving car and the car stops, respects
the bird's little life. The wind lifts the litter and dumps it
on my lawn. My lawn, the last plant I haven't killed.

Sand flies into my face when I turn to the ocean.
Two lovers yell at each other. Is it out of anger,
or just to be heard over the water's giant crash?
I hover behind them, grasping for some sentence
to break through the noise, to be a revelation.

Angela, I know you can't hear me from New York
but if you could, I would be muttering, "What the fuck,
what the *fuck.*" I overheard the bag lady repeating,
"No one could die for you." I think that's true. Except
for maybe you, Angela, but I would never ask you to.
You are always so kind to me, despite my solipsism.

I remember a stranger once touching my chest, telling
me I had a strong heart. I didn't laugh. Are we only
as strong as what we can hold? Some elephants can carry
twice their body weight. Once I carried my lover's television
outside and vaulted it to the curb. Nearly broke my back.

Some people can love so easily that they could
cuddle a shark tank. Angela, I think you are one
of those people. What is the exact distance
between us? Miles as measurement seems false,
but hours pass and pass. We do not speak.

The daylight unbuttons itself to show its big dark
belly freckled with stars. Angela, your baby
is nine days late. I told you I would call
but I can't right now. There is an eager line
of taxis honking for me on the street. The barges'
baritone offering far out on the bay. What can I offer back?

I can't call now, can't call, but you call me instead,
say, "I'm bored" over the noise, and I tell you
how my shelf collapsed. How my lover asked
me to shave his back. You laugh and laugh.
What else can I give to this world?

DO THIS, DO THAT

It's Valentine's Day and the server
sets our table, her arms cross-hatched
with scars. I've never hated
myself enough to do that, really
cut, but I'd be lying if I said I
never tried or wished I could.

I don't know if I would stop
letting others hurt me if I had
the power. Perhaps for her it
is the kind of pain she can control,
not the unexpected lash from
an external force, some cut
about erratic driving.

I never thought the face
of pain would serve me, offer me
food despite its own suffering.
But yet I can always locate it,
ask it for a little more, do this, do that,
another cup of soup, another slap
across the ass that means *it's here and real.*
My chair pushes up against me, tender.

Please, hand me a topological menu
of the inner universe, the *Idiot's Guide*
to What We are Able to Tolerate.
Allow me to ask her how
it got that far, her body that beat up
for what?

There are some risks
which we are willing to fall
hard against—a thin blade,
a lover's hand—in hopes we
find some better place to sit
with them, a table with a candle,
a lover stroking a healing arm,
a server with a familiar smile asking,
once again, Can I take
your order?

ANOTHER REPORT

Sometimes I think I'm better off
keeping my mouth shut. Other times
I open up and hope something good

falls in—a sleeping pill, a flower petal
soft as the wing of a moth. I hope for
a moth to fly in through the crack in the glass.

For the glass to uncrack, unrest to surrender.
It's too late to revive the sheep. I mean to say
I've barely slept all week, still thinking

about the fur shell of a dead squirrel
full of maggots I found in the backyard.
I had to hold the thing,

lift it with a rake and wrap it
in a shopping bag. I threw it in the dumpster,
the body light and warm with stench.

Something parasitic remains in you
when you handle certain matters.
It makes you want to remove

what lingers and put it in the ground.
I gave the rake to the neighbors,
and avoided the backyard, even after

winter when the crows crowded the trees and cried.
I closed for business. I gave up
whatever I had that felt like it was dying on me—

an old cactus in a teacup, my dumb guitar,
the facial expressions for *thanks* and *I don't think so.*
I left a friend that year.

I stopped calling my mother
because who needs the same bad advice
you'd already give to yourself?

Once she told me to *write it all down*
and look where that has gotten me.

EVERYONE IS SMILING

There is no good reason.
The sun shrugs from behind
the fog. But everyone
is smiling! I look down
at the sidewalk. Still,
the faces of strangers
cannot be avoided,
their cute mouths curved upwards
and their arms swinging
like happy ropes. I groan
at the sky. I walk by the balloon shop,
past the pack of nannies
pushing carriages bubbling
over with babies. Hoping the mood
might come over me, I go to
the pet store, hold a puppy.
I have two beers at the Squat
'n Gobble. I have the pie—delicious—
but it doesn't fix the day. I have
no idea why everyone is smiling.
There must be something
in the water. Something in my hair.
On my face. Frantic for a mirror,
I crash into the waiter on my way
to the bathroom. He spills two sodas
and a plate of chicken wings.
I'm sorry, I'm sorry,
barbecue sauce on my knees.
And what does he do but laugh?
Why is this mess funny?
He tells me it's all you can do

in these moments, but now someone
has to wait for their wings. I scan
the room for an agitated face, but
nothing. Everyone is smiling
into their coffee, out the window,
smiling at their newspapers and at
their friends. It's like at this minute,
everyone is filled with joy
or the world's best chicken.
It leaves us in a state of inexplicable
bliss, every mouth softening into sweetness:
we are good, we are happy,
we have wings.

III.

Lift up your face, my love. Lift up your mouth.

—Muriel Rukeyser

THE ONLY ONE YOU'LL EVER

Darling, I have made you an omelet.
I have taken out the trash for you.

I will not wake you. I will walk the dog
for you and for you, I will wait

in the car while you run into the store—
you'll just be a minute—and ten minutes

later I still love you. I love your cold
hands up my shirt when you get home

from work and I love that you work
at the bagel shop. I love your bagels.

You smell like scallions and garlic
and your shoes are the shoes

of a humble man. Your brown dusty shoes
next to my brown dusty shoes

at the foot of our bed, the untied laugh
of shoes. We laugh in bed when the dog

licks our toes in the morning, and I laugh
when you speak into my bare chest

in a Darth Vader voice and tell me you love me.
You tell me you love me when we fight

about the thermostat or who spent more on groceries
and I fight a little less with you, I soften

and cry, and when I cry, you stop
your yelling. You stop smiling when I tell you

what to do or how to fold the towels, and I
am working on that. You are working on

chivalry and I appreciate your efforts. You open
my car door on the way to the dollar store and I feel like

a fucking princess. It takes very little
to please me, and I am pleased

that you have acknowledged my new red dress.
You also look very nice, a little wild, always

combing your hair against its natural part,
your flamboyant exclamation of hair.

I say, "Let's touch base later about dinner"
and you say, "I'll always touch

your base." We drink beer in the park
and eat ice cream in the dark. Together,

we peel mangoes. Together, we get out of
the car to look at the fat orange

moon dipping itself into the dark fondue of trees,
the sky so vast, it silences us. Sometimes I worry

when we're this quiet. "We're in this together,"
I say, and you say, "How about we just be quiet

for a minute." How about you just count
the stars, and I will connect the dots

between them.

OLD LOAF

The bread crumbled
all over my floor, a crunchy sea
of stale. Sometimes I worry that this
is all there is. Won't you come over,
bring some soft rolls to calm my nerves,
some garlic oil? We can eat together tonight.
Godless, yes—but I have wine and cable.

IN THE INSECT ROOM

We kissed on the Tornado.
You made me let the cow lick my hand.
Its tongue slapped my wrist: live wet meat.
In the insect room, two dragonflies mating,
pinned to purple poster board.

The scattered midway crowd
could not unstick our candied clasp.
Soda spilled between my toes
like powdered dirt, confectioner's silt.
We did pull fried dough
apart from opposite ends.
You did not win me a giant panda.

ADULT DATING

You disengaged my bra with infrared
precision in the dark, then kicked your boots
into the trench between your wall and bed.
Your sheets reminded me of parachutes

ballooning on my head. My purity
was not at stake—nor were my underwear,
apparently. Into obscurity they went,
but neither of us seemed to care.

Initially, the way two people jive
can turn into a hot catastrophe,
but we buzzed until we shook the beehive—
I puddled into pulverized debris.

We faked our sleep, and learned the lexicon
of subtle signals surreptitiously
while knotting in an awkward hexagon
and kicking one another viciously.

The morning clashed with last night's chardonnay,
uncorked and mocking on the countertop.
Quickly, you had me on my way
to A and Third, the nearest subway stop.

HOME IMPROVEMENT

They are tearing up the sidewalk outside
your house, the jackhammer hired

by some rich neighbor, likely the one
with the lemon tree where the dumb

birds blab and cluster
around the feeder,

shitting all over your car,
pecking at the yard

for some scrap of something left
over, a fallen seed, the rest

of someone's lunch.
How they seem to get so much

from nothing. You doubt your rich
neighbors are sitting on their couch

like you are, wearing industrial earmuffs
and eating a bitter sandwich alone. Enough

with all this need for improvement.
You never noticed the crack in the cement

and you otherwise might consider
being outside right now, enjoying the weather.

But instead you're left to explore
the split linoleum, the broken chair,

all that's been unattended.
There's also your temper, the upset friend,

your intent to stop complaining in the office
before 5:30. No one will miss

your sarcasm. At least a little nod
from the cop when you curb your dog,

at least now you're trying. The list
is long, and it's likely that you'll miss

a lot. Maybe start with a birdhouse
in a lemon tree, a lemon mousse

for your neighbor. Maybe save a pile
of the broken sidewalk for a little while.

Might be able to make something
from nothing.

UTOPIA, TEXAS

My first trip to Texas
and we drove four hours out
into the hill country
where jackrabbits launched
themselves across the narrow roads
and the live oaks widened along
the long miles.

We ate gourmet off paper plates
and stumbled upon a real rodeo
where a Chihuahua chased the steer
through the pulverized dirt
and the children clung to the backs
of sheep bolting from the chute.

I was wide-eyed watching the young boys
raise and lower their hands in time
with the kicking ass of the maddened cattle,
choreography older than any living bull.

Everyone hollering from the bleachers,
everything softening into the dusty light.

I sang softly in the car back
to our room on the Sabinal
where we fucked in the river.

A golden retriever named Stevie Wonder.
I couldn't have imagined it better.

Who cared, then, what we didn't know
about each other—the Texas landscape dimmed
fast into the darkening sky, and all the people
we've ever loved went on living without us.

MILAGRO

Here's a fact: a pendant pulled
from his pocket, dull and silver.

A heart shape, a shovel.

Vena cava, I'd like to let you burn
me. Let's try fire external.

A comet on my skin. I like
your scorch, your irresistible blister. Faster

than fate, it's the weight of you, star of my sternum,
your local pulse, a third degree pressure.

O arc of back, small of back! Neck, the dark
angle of groin and last, the internal lack.

It's metaphor and fact. Like this:

the weekend in the cabin, cold as shit,
the firewood he stole and set and didn't tend,

the fight and then another fight,
the embedded splinter still surfacing,

the trace of something burning
still hanging in the air—

SWEET NOTHING

what little slit   there is   to show for it
a purse within a purse   darling   I'll bet
not every man can tingle   like a girl
with more nerve endings   who needs to seem
engaged   the man   wanting more   giving
persists   how come   I can't perceive my own
organ   cistern   stall of   infant chances
existence itself   o speculum
the modest light   exposing one exact
introverting   glimpse to another
individual   who asks about
my calendar of bleeding   the number of lovers
someday it will stop   all this wetness
so much there is to say   for it   nothing

OLYMPIA

—*after Manet*

I'm not even looking
at the basket or the cat.
I might pet it with my dangling
shoe and then what?

The maid Matilde worries
about my breasts out bare
but I will not regret it.
Five days straight I'm here

and his mouth hardly moves!
No look could match
his measured glances.
He only tells me not to stare

but I take that as a dare.
When he's back
behind the easel, I rarely
tire. I finger my wrap

and then retie my hair.
His brush taps like a bullet
of sweat onto a sheet
pulled taut. He might hope

I hope for him to drag
his hand along the summit
of my hip, pull the ribbon
from my neck. If he does that,

my head might drop.
His foot steps back.
The air drapes us
with sweat and oil, pale

paint everywhere. I memorize
his sigh and find the scent
of wildflowers. He groans
as if his day has been

an uphill climb against
the whole world's fastest men.
He wants to end, but I'm not done
imagining I'm the mountain.

GEMINI

Infinite embryos, mortal mother
raped by swan. Twins, immoral and kissing.

Fantastic prophylactics for
unparallel axes. As in mixing milk

with marrow, sealing stone with cement.
Semen, simultaneously born, still

bonding. Kin skin touching. Unopposed
chromosomes, man & man coupling.

Secret reprises, repressed caresses. Careening
through bedsheets of gods and men,

brothers, covertly conjoining. The joy.
The irreparable coveting.

SAME ROOM

when there was no more soup you would
go to the store oh
wait for the day of the last slaughtered cow

go to the sand on the dustiest beach
cover your flamboyant nose
ankledeep in seaweed

my hot monkey sundancing
the tarantella 'til the damp sweat darkens your new long hair

I've baked you the basic apple
eat because it cannot speak for itself

I'm suggesting a return to body
a corporeal overhaul of the handless the faceless the otherwise
unnamed friends we make in the safe abacus
of our collective cerebellum

we love the same loneliness we are in the same room

thank you for saying there are many ways of saying
rooster ways of being woken
and places to call womb

*

May you never be flummoxed, love,
whiplashed or otherwise whitewashed—
your brick wall red rises before the sun does.
Let nothing outlast your best construction, the only
wish you want for it, *so long lives this*
and all that shit. I'll let you think that
once you had a body and *remember not*
the hand that writ it
but know that I think body
is the only home.

BIG TOP

Two trapeze wires, twisted. Twins
rising from a tangled fall.
A bearded lady, too sad to kiss for quarters.

The circus might not weigh enough
to hold itself down in the tornado.
Yet the elephant bets it will stay put, and it does.

GOODBYE, MILWAUKEE

To my landlord,
your delicate wife—
I am sorry about my dog,
your rug. I will send
you a new rug from China!
I might go to China!
I might go to Maine!
So goodbye, Milwaukee
and your decadent eggburgers,
your skinny-legged trot to the truck
in the early flurries, the truck bed,
your pickups and takeouts,
goodbye to your high school
high fives. Goodbye to my hometown!
I made it out alive! I survived
every late night at the Hi Dive,
three shots, four beers
and five bucks at the jukebox—
Ain't Too Proud to Beg
but I don't have to,
there's some drummer
from Detroit buying me another,
brushing my hair aside.
Goodbye to my twenties!
My youthful thighs!
I had plenty of time! I had plenty
of French fries, too, fried pickles,
fried jalapenos, fried zucchini, fried olives,
chicken fried steak, triple-fried chicken,
the dazzling deep-fried blossoming onion,
and I'll have the halibut, pan fried.

Dear sausage, goodbye.
I have known for some time.
Dear summer thigh sweat,
gym treadmills, the elevator guy—
dear 2125 Prospect Avenue,
goodbye. I love you. I'm leaving.
There's a box of your t-shirts
on your back porch and you can
drop off the year 2000 any time.

NOT REALLY

Another kitten collage
at the vet—how cute.
I flirt with the technician.
My dog hides under
the metal table.
I don't blame him.

No one wants a thermometer
up their butt, even if it means
feeling better later. I'm not feeling
any better about the sparrow
my dog ate or all those clothes
in my closet covered in fur.

You would think
that a closet is a great place
to hide, but after a few hours
it feels like you're shrinking.

You would think
someone would notice. No one
knocked down the door
after three days straight
of sitting in bed eating nachos.

I've had enough contact
for one week, enough nachos
for a lifetime. My dog is enough.

Enough lives in my life, so exhausting.

All my life, I'm either showing up
or shying away. Shaking hands
or taking off. Every day,
my dog drags me around the lake,
investigates the bushes as if something
has happened there. Could be
a bagel or a dead bird.

Could be something that should
be found, a pigeon feather
or a razor blade.

Both glimmer in the glance
of the sun. You can't hide
from that kind of witness.

LAYOVER

Outside, they're salting the tarmac
while I pull tinsel from my hairbrush
in the restroom and inspect my teeth
with the tinsel. A flush crescendos
in the background. Another woman
steps up to the mirror in the anti-bacterial air.

It's another year.

A tiny spider drops from the ceiling
on its invisible line, pausing midair before
it continues to descend, no big rush
for the imminent water spout, the sweet wet
fast track to the afterlife. Everyone pauses
here, gathers at a gate and waits
to be lifted, luggage, miniature dachshunds and all,
guitar cases shifting in takeoff upwards and through
the cumulonimbus mass that straddles
the greater metropolitan area of Minneapolis.

The lights of the terminal ignore the fact of 9:30 p.m.
and sparrows circle the inside ceiling of the food court
like the way airplanes must skim
the inner atmosphere. I wonder if I will ever fly
past it, beyond the window seat
 of a slightly curved horizon. They have
airplanes that can do that now, but I don't know
what I would learn about my life by being so far away
from where I live it. Maybe not knowing
is enough of a reason to do it: there,
an entire weather system, there, the Great Salt Lake.
Look, that is our planet and beyond it, a vast black
expanse of nothing, of night.

Two hours delayed, and I've already
eaten all my peanuts. There are still no seats
at the gate. A group of people fill
the airport bar, leaning into their drinks
like horses to a pond, their eyes soft and blank.
At any moment at least two men will tumble
to the ground, a game on the widescreen that is sure
to end badly for someone. The server is nowhere.
I just wanted the Cobb salad, a mindless trip.
I wanted to start the year off right.

VANISHING POINT

I might be obsessed
with smallness. Sometimes
I want to yell "MACARONI!"
but then I feel void of meaning.
How about you give me meaning
and vice versa. How about
you're the doctor and I'm your
subject. I want your subject
to like my subject. I like
your mouth but I can't hear
a word you're saying. I'm just saying,
if existence were an endless line,
a heart monitor, you might be my biggest
blip. I might be a crater. I might be
wrong. Last wrong turn
I ended up in Dubuque
on the world's shortest trolley.
At the top of the hill, I could still
see my green flip-flops melting
into the asphalt. They were small,
very small. Perspective
is a big deal. It's as big
as a baby's arm. It's bigger than
the bones they found buried
beneath the old drive-in theatre.
I remember making out there
in the back seat: your hands,
my green soccer shorts. I remember
the shorts! It's always the little things.
A man carves a Marilyn Monroe
so small that she fits in the eye

of a needle. No needle will prevent you
from shrinking entirely. It appears
you are becoming smaller
from here, in The Future.
I think you had blue eyes.
I can't see your face from this distance.
You appear to be merging with
the tree down the street.

ACKNOWLEDGMENTS

"Same Room" quotes lines from Shakespeare's *Sonnets 18 and 71*

"No Answer" adapts a line from *The Little Prince* by Antoine de Saint Exupéry

"Goodbye, Milwaukee" borrows lines from Kenneth Koch's poem "To My Twenties"

"Vanishing Point" borrows language from the 1990 movie *Pump Up the Volume*

Many thanks to the following journals in which versions of these poems previously appeared: *236*, *Best New Poets 2008*, *Best New Poets 2010*, *The Carolina Quarterly*, *Circus Book*, *Connotation Press: An Online Artifact*, *Failbetter*, *Five Points*, *La Petite Zine*, *Midday Moon*, *The Minnesota Review*, *MiPoesias*, *The National Poetry Review*, *The New Ohio Review*, *No Tell Motel*, *Pine Hills Review*, *The Red Wheelbarrow Review*, *Selfies In Ink*, *Sewanee Theological Review*, *Sparkle and Blink* and *Unpleasant Event Schedule*.

This book is also dedicated to Angela Basile, who has provided insight, inspiration and encouragement when I needed it most.

I am indebted to the generosity from The Tin House Writers' Workshop, The Dorothy Sargent Rosenberg Fund, Boston University and Ohio University for their support of my work.

Kim Addonizio was instrumental in seeing these poems (and me) reach their full potential—for that, I am grateful. Special thanks to all of my teachers, especially Mark Halliday, Mark Wunderlich, Janis Butler Holm, Erin Belieu, Rosanna Warren and Robert Pinsky. Also, thank you to David Dodd Lee for his tireless efforts on behalf of my manuscript, and his enthusiasm in general for my poetry.

Enormous gratitude for those who offered valuable critical insight during the assembly of this manuscript: Alicia Jo Rabins, Dana Jaye Cadman, Brock Guthrie and Brooke Champagne.

I want to offer my thanks to friends and editors who invested themselves in me and my poetry over the years: Daniel Nester, John Hoppenthaler, Jessica Conner, Ben Foss, Emily Knight, Melinda Blockorby, Bob Dickerson, Cheryl Davis, Tresha Faye Haefner, Jasper Haze, Leila Chatti, Jennifer Drew, Sarah Strickley, Ashley Capps, Carrie Oeding, Melissa Tuckey, Meghan Tally, Kelly Voet, Robert Wohlers, Michael Russem, Betsy Hogan, and my best critic and brother, Shane Knapp.

And lastly, love to Jennifer Skovan Santiago for seeing the light in me before it fully shined.

Photo: In Her Image Photography

Tracey Knapp works in graphic design and communications in
San Francisco. She received graduate degrees in creative writing
and English from Boston University and Ohio University, where she
taught literature, composition and creative writing. She has received
scholarships from The Tin House Writers' Workshop and
The Dorothy Rosenberg Poetry Fund.